CONTENTS

KV-106-328

Acknowledgements

The author and publishers wish to thank the following who have kindly given permission for the use of copyright material:

Librarie Armand Colin for extract from *The Weimar Republic* by J. Hiden; David Higham Associates Ltd on behalf of Kitty Hart for extract from *Return to Auschwitz*, Sidgwick & Jackson (1981); Hutchinson Publishing Group Ltd for extract 'I Knew Hitler' by Kurt Ludecke in *Purnell's History of the Twentieth Century*; Hutchinson Publishing Group Ltd for extract 'Deux Nuits sans Jour' by Dr Sulyok in *Purnell's History of the Twentieth Century*; Laurence Pollinger Ltd, London, on behalf of Richard Hanser for extract from *Prelude to Terror* (1971); Martin Secker and Warburg Ltd and Simon & Schuster Inc. for extract from *The Rise and Fall of the Third Reich* by William Shirer, © 1959, 1960 by William L. Shirer, reprinted by permission of Simon & Schuster Inc.; University of Exeter for extracts from *Nazism 1919–1945*, vols 1 (1983) and 2 (1984), edited by J. Noakes and G. Pridham.

The author and publishers wish to acknowledge, with thanks, the following photographic sources:

Barnaby's Picture Library pp 40, 50; BBC Hulton Picture Library pp 8, 42; Bilderdienst Süddeutscher Verlag pp 16, 23, 25, 29, 30, 31, 38, 44, 46, 49, 53, 55; cartoons supplied by permission of *The London Standard* pp 28, 39; The Photo Source p 33; Picturepoint p 52; Popperfoto pp 7, 15, 45 (t); John Topham Picture Library p 34 (t); The Wiener Library p 11; Ullstein pp 6, 10, 13, 24, 34 (b), 47.

The publishers have made every effort to trace copyright holders, but if they have inadvertently overlooked any, they will be pleased to make the necessary arrangements at the first opportunity.

PREFACE

The study of history is exciting, whether in a good story well told, a mystery solved by the judicious unravelling of clues, or a study of the men, women and children whose fears and ambitions, successes and tragedies make up the collective memory of mankind.

This series aims to reveal this excitement to pupils through a set of topic books on important historical subjects from the Middle Ages to the present day. Each book contains four main elements: a narrative and descriptive text, lively and relevant illustrations, extracts of contemporary evidence, and questions for further thought and work. Involvement in these elements should provide an adventure which will bring the past to life in the imagination of the pupil.

Each book is also designed to develop the knowledge, skills and concepts so essential to a pupil's growth. It provides a wide, varying introduction to the evidence available on each topic. In handling this evidence, pupils will increase their understanding of basic historical concepts such as causation and change, as well as of more advanced ideas such as revolution and democracy. In addition, their use of basic study skills will be complemented by more sophisticated historical skills such as the detection of bias and the formulation of opinion.

The intended audience for the series is pupils of eleven to sixteen years: it is expected that the earlier topics will be introduced in the first three years of secondary school, while the nineteenth and twentieth century topics are directed towards first examinations.

HISTORY IN DEPTH

THE RISE AND FALL OF HITLER'S GERMANY

Simon Williams

Deputy Head of Grey Court School,
Richmond, Surrey

MACMILLAN

For Joanna and Charlotte

First published in 1986
Reprinted 1987 (twice), 1988, 1989

Published by
MACMILLAN EDUCATION LTD
Houndmills, Basingstoke, Hampshire RG21 2XS
and London
Companies and representatives
throughout the world

Printed in Hong Kong

British Library Cataloguing in Publication Data
Williams, Simon
The Rise and Fall of Hitler's Germany—(History in Depth)
1. Nationalsozialistische Deutsche Arbeiter–Partei
—History
I. Title II. Series
324.234'038   DD253.25
ISBN 0–333–38711–2

Author's acknowledgements
I would like to thank the following for their contributions to this
book: Christine Allford for typing the manuscript; the staff of the
Wiener Library, London, and my brother Nicholas for their
advice, comments and suggestions, and my wife Daphne for her
support throughout.

1 THE EARLY YEARS OF THE NAZI PARTY

When the news broke that Germany had declared war first on Russia and then on France in early August 1914, there were scenes of joy throughout the German Empire as strangers linked arms to celebrate and sing what became the new national anthem, *Deutschland, Deutschland über Alles* ('Germany, Germany, above all else'). More than four years later the scene in Germany was completely different. The war was still continuing: 2.4 million German soldiers had been killed on the battlefield, while inside Germany 750 000 people had died of starvation as a result of the British naval blockade. On 10 November 1918 the German Empire collapsed as the Kaiser fled to Holland. The following day the rulers of the new republic signed the armistice and seven months later, under threat of an invasion from the wartime Allies, Britain, France and the United States, they were forced to sign the Treaty of Versailles which quickly became known in Germany as the 'Treaty of Shame'.

Kaiser: the German emperor

Main points of the Treaty of Versailles

1 *German war-guilt* The aggression of Germany and its allies caused the war. Therefore they had to pay compensation (reparations) to the allied victors for damage resulting from the war.

2 *German loss of land* Germany lost 13 per cent of its territory in Europe, including Alsace-Lorraine and the Polish Corridor, and all its colonies in Africa, China and the Pacific.

3 *German armed forces* The German army was limited to 100 000. No tanks, aircraft or U-boats were allowed. Allied forces were to occupy the Rhineland for 15 years and no German troops were to be stationed on either side of the River Rhine. In addition, Germany was forbidden to unite with Austria.

The birth of the Party

The Weimar Republic, named after the town in Germany where the new constitution was drawn up in 1919, had got off to a bad start. Many Germans blamed the new government for betraying their country, arguing, quite wrongly, that the army could have continued the war had it not been 'stabbed in the back' by those who had signed the armistice. Nationalist groups sprang up all over the country,

5

Germans, young and old, protest against the Treaty of Versailles

pledged to save the German Fatherland both from the democratic politicians who were now in power and from the German Communists who were threatening to seize power. One such group was the German Workers' Party founded in 1919 by a Munich railway worker, Anton Drexler.

Drexler had been impressed by a speech made from the floor at one of the poorly attended meetings of the new party. He invited the

Europe after the peace settlement

Key:
- Demilitarised Rhineland
- Territory lost by Germany
- Austro-Hungarian empire until 1918
- Former territory of Imperial Russia

speaker, a youngish man named Adolf Hitler, to attend the next committee meeting. Hitler went out of curiosity, finding his way into the back room of a shabby restaurant where a few members of the committee were sitting round the table which was lit by a broken gas lamp. The Party had 7 marks 50 pfennigs to its credit, no political programme, no leaflets and not even a rubber stamp. It was a depressing meeting, Hitler recalled afterwards, but two days later he decided to join. The Party shared many of his ideas and it was small enough for him to take over. Hitler's decision to enter politics had momentous results. Fourteen years later 13 million Germans had voted for his party and Hitler, as the new Chancellor of Germany, stood poised to smash the democratic Weimar Republic he hated so intensely.

Hitler's early years

Hitler's rise was all the more remarkable in view of the setbacks of his early life. Born in 1889, the son of an Austrian customs official, Hitler did badly at secondary school and at the age of 18 left for Vienna, determined to become an artist. Twice he applied to take the entrance exam to the Academy of Fine Arts and twice he was turned down because his samples of work were not good enough. His money ran out and he sank into poverty; he was forced to give up his rented apartment room for a bed in a men's hostel. Moody and friendless, he eked out a living by selling his own copies of pictures of Vienna to dealers and engravers. In 1913 he left Vienna for Munich and a year later he was fighting for Germany in the Great War.

Hitler (ringed) among the huge Munich crowd celebrating the outbreak of war on 1 August 1914

The war gave Hitler the chance to escape from poverty and failure. He lived dangerously and fought with courage, being awarded medals for bravery which included the rare distinction of the Iron Cross (First Class). But his new found sense of purpose in life was shattered when he heard the news of Germany's collapse as he lay in hospital recovering his sight after a British gas attack.

To Hitler, Germany's surrender was further proof of the Jewish master-plan for world conquest. Searching for scapegoats to explain his own failure in Vienna before the war, Hitler had hungrily swallowed the crude anti-Semitism (hostility towards the Jews) of the gutter press. He returned to Munich after the war, convinced, along with many other German nationalists, that the Weimar democrats and the Communist revolutionaries were part of a sinister Jewish plot to overthrow the German race. These fanatical beliefs would not have altered the course of history had not Hitler possessed exceptional political talents which he finally turned to use at the age of 30 when he decided to join the German Workers' Party.

Political success

Hitler quickly changed the German Workers' Party from a run-down debating club into an organisation that had mass support in Munich. He was a spell-binding public speaker and thousands flocked to his meetings to hear him attack the targets of nationalist fury: the Weimar politicians, the treaty-makers of Versailles, the Communists and, above all, the Jews. Hitler kept the message simple and played on the emotions of his audience. In his speeches he started slowly, gradually working himself and the audience up into a state of anger against the 'enemies' of Germany before reaching a climax with his appeal for unity to save the German Fatherland. After a two-hour volley of words, Hitler left the rostrum soaking in sweat while the crowd poured out into the night singing patriotic songs and shouting anti-Semitic slogans.

Hitler, the street politician, acknowledges his uniformed supporters

By 1923 Hitler was in absolute control of the Party, now renamed the National Socialist German Workers' Party, or Nazi Party. It had its own 25 point programme, its own distinctive emblem of the swastika, a party newspaper and a private army – the brown-shirted storm-troopers or SA who controlled the streets of Munich.

The country was in the grip of a serious crisis which had been triggered off in January 1923 when French troops marched into the Ruhr to seize its coal-mines and iron and steel works in place of the reparations which Germany had failed to deliver to France. For the first time since 1914 Germany was united again in protest against the French occupation, and the Weimar government supported a general strike of all workers in the Ruhr. With the industrial heartland of Germany at a standstill, the government resorted to printing more money in order to increase its revenue.

Printing presses worked round the clock to churn out paper money, with the result that prices rose astronomically. In two weeks a loaf of bread went up in price from 1.8 billion marks to 32 billion marks. Workers were paid twice a day; using baskets and wheelbarrows to carry their money, they rushed out to shop while their wages could still buy goods. Many went hungry as farmers refused to sell food in exchange for worthless paper money. Those who had put money aside over the years found that the value of their savings had been wiped out and many pensioners were plunged into acute poverty.

The government resigned and the new Chancellor, Gustav Stresemann, called off the campaign in the Ruhr and handed over the reparations to France. This humiliating defeat for the government convinced Hitler that the time was ripe to march on Berlin and overthrow the Republic. His own party was not strong enough to succeed on its own. He needed the support of Kahr, Lossow and Seisser, who were in control of the Bavarian government and hostile to the Weimar Republic. At first Hitler was confident he had their support, but then they began to hesitate so Hitler decided to force their hand.

The Beer Hall Putsch

On 8 November 1923 Kahr was addressing an audience in one of Munich's larger beer cellars when suddenly Hitler, flanked by SA men, burst into the meeting. He jumped on a table, fired his pistol in the air and shouted, 'The National Revolution has begun'. He ordered Kahr, Lossow and Seisser into a side room where he tried to persuade them to back his plan. They finally agreed, but only after General Ludendorff, the legendary hero of the Great War, had arrived and pledged his support. However, in the early hours of the following morning it became clear to Hitler that Kahr and his colleagues had turned against him. In desperation Hitler decided to march into the centre of Munich in the hope of rallying the people of the city to his side.

At 11 a.m. on 9 November some 3000 Nazis, led by Hitler and Ludendorff, set off in military order for the town centre. There was no trouble until the police blocked their way at the end of a narrow street. Somebody fired a shot which was followed by a volley of shots from both sides, leaving 16 Nazis and three policemen dead. As the firing continued, Ludendorff marched on to the square beyond, where he was arrested. Hitler fell to the ground and then escaped from the scene by car. He later claimed that he behaved with great courage, but his enemies argued that all he was concerned about was saving his own life. What did happen after the firing started?

The march through Munich

Using the evidence: Hitler — a hero or a coward?

A *The witnesses agree that Hitler was the first to get up, run backwards and drive away whilst hundreds of his comrades were still lying on the ground. They were not lying there defenceless; they had fired. The battle was not decided.*
Konrad Heiden: *Hitler*, 1936

Schultze: Hitler's driver

B *Hitler painfully struggled to his feet, cradling his injured arm. He was in agony as he slowly moved away from the battleground, face pale, hair falling over his face. He and Schultze came upon a small boy lying at the curb bleeding profusely. Hitler wanted to carry him off but Schultze called to his wife's cousin to take the boy . . . they finally reached Hitler's old grey Selve . . . Hitler told the driver to head for the beer cellar so he could find out what was going on.*
John Toland: *Hitler*, 1976

C *Though Hitler was not the first to flee the scene of battle, as some chroniclers have it, he did not exactly cover himself with glory. He had plunged to the pavement at the first volley, stayed there until the shooting was over, and made off as soon as opportunity offered. At no point did he behave heroically . . . it was therefore necessary to invent something . . . the story was that as he threaded his way among the dead bodies while the bullets were still flying, he saw a little boy who had somehow wandered into the line of fire. The Führer, without hesitation and despite the excruciating pain of his shoulder, picked up the lad and wrapped his arms around him protectively (not an easy thing to do with only one arm in working order). He then carried the child to safety before he thought of his own.*
Richard Hanser: *Prelude to Terror*, 1971

Führer: the title assumed by Hitler in 1934. It means 'leader'

D *And this is Adolf Hitler, who tells everybody that he will one day seize power, who was lying flat on his belly in front of the Feldherrnhalle [a building in Munich near the shooting] and who crawled into the bed of Hanfstaengl [a leading Nazi who gave Hitler refuge after his escape]. He already has a nine-room flat, a villa, three cars and a whip. He guarantees cheap labour and high wages, high prices for grain and cheap bread. Whoever is ill can seek his help with complete confidence!*
Social Democrats' election poster, 1932

1 Write down what each of the four sources states Hitler did after the firing started.
2 Which of the sources presents Hitler's action in
   a) the most favourable light
   b) the most unfavourable light.
   Explain the reasons for your answer.
3 Heiden was living in Germany at the time of the putsch and managed to speak to witnesses. Does that mean that his account, source **A**, is more likely to be true?
4 Hitler won several medals for bravery during the Great War. Does that suggest that source **B** is more likely to be accurate?
5 Suggest two reasons to explain why the sources give such a totally different view of what happened. What other information about the sources might help you decide which account is most likely to be accurate?
6 In what way do the picture and the words in the election poster support each other in their view of Hitler?
7 Why was the question of what Hitler did after the firing started so important to both Hitler and his opponents? Refer to sources **C** and **D** in your answer.
8 Referring to the evidence on page II, do you think it is true that the historian's task is hopeless since he or she can never be sure of what actually did happen in the past?

After the putsch

The march to Berlin had not got beyond Munich, yet Hitler was quick to recover from the fiasco of the Beer Hall Putsch. Two days after his escape he was arrested, but at his trial he turned the tables on Kahr, Lossow and Seisser, the chief prosecution witnessess, claiming that he was the true German patriot and they were the traitors. For attempting to overthrow the government Hitler was given a five year sentence of which he served only nine months. While in prison he wrote the first volume of his autobiography *Mein Kampf* ('My Struggle') and pondered over the future. He became convinced that the road to power lay in winning votes at elections rather than violent revolution.

However, by the elections of 1928, Germany's economic situation had changed. Having recovered from the disastrous inflation of 1923, industrial production had doubled and real wages had risen by a third. In the elections more than 70 per cent of the German people voted for parties that supported the Republic. In the summer of 1929 Hitler was, in the words of one historian, 'no more than the leader of a small splinter party, scarcely known outside Bavaria and very likely doomed to remain for ever on the periphery of political life'.

2 HITLER'S RISE TO POWER

Depression

Between 1924 and 1929 foreign money poured into German factories convincing many observers that the Weimar Republic had fully recovered from the crisis of 1923. But Gustav Stresemann, Germany's Foreign Secretary from 1924 to 1929, realised that the country's prosperity depended on loans from abroad which could be withdrawn at any time. In 1929 he warned his fellow countrymen that 'Germany is dancing on a volcano'. In the same year the volcano erupted when American investors suddenly panicked and rushed to sell their shares on Wall Street, the centre of the American stock market. Share prices tumbled, investors withdrew their money from abroad and within a short space of time many factories were at a standstill and millions were out of work.

The effects of the Wall Street Crash were felt across the world, but Germany was worst hit as it depended more on foreign loans than the other industrial nations. By 1932 nearly one in three of all German workers was unemployed.

The Weimar politicians seemed to have no answer to the worsening crisis. Chancellor Bruning was determined that the government should not spend any more money than it was receiving in taxes. But as trade fell and unemployment rose, Bruning had less money coming into the treasury and more to pay out in unemployment benefits. To balance the books, he raised taxes, cut the salaries of government workers and reduced unemployment benefits. In 1930, in protest against this last measure, the Socialists withdrew from the coalition which had governed Germany for the last two years. To carry on his government, Bruning now had to rely on President Hindenburg's support under Article 48 of the Weimar Constitution which gave the President special powers in an emergency.

The move to extremes

As the dole queues lengthened and Germany slid deeper into depression, more and more voters turned to political parties which rejected the Weimar Republic and offered their own brands of dictatorship. To the Communists, the Great Depression was final proof that the capitalist system was collapsing as banks, businesses and governments in all the capitalist countries failed to provide work and to get their economies back on the move. It was only a matter of time, the Communists argued, before they would sweep to power in Germany and elsewhere, armed with the mass support of the working class.

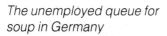

The unemployed queue for soup in Germany

13

This seemed to be happening in Germany as increasing numbers of workers switched their support from the Socialists to the Communists.

Between 1928 and 1933 the increase in the support for the Nazi Party was even more spectacular than that of the Communists. Hitler blamed the Weimar politicians for the Depression. They had signed the Treaty of Versailles; they had bled Germany by handing over reparations and now all they could do was squabble among themselves as the nation sank deeper into the mire. Hitler promised he would end the squabbling and unite the country by destroying its 'enemies' within. Then Germany would be strong enough to stand up to its 'enemies' abroad and could tear up the hated Treaty of Versailles.

The Depression did much of Hitler's work for him by making large numbers of Germans from all classes dissatisfied with the present and nervous about the future. The factory workers bore the brunt of unemployment with 40 per cent of all male workers out of a job by 1932. Shopkeepers and traders struggled to make ends meet as people had less to spend on food, clothes and other items. Many of Germany's two million farmers were heavily in debt as the price of food dropped sharply. Most Germans who owned property, whether it was a small corner shop or a large factory, a three acre farm or a huge estate in the country, were terrified that the Communists would come to power and seize whatever they owned.

The saviour of Germany

Hitler cleverly played on all these grievances and fears, knowing that the road to power lay in winning as many votes as possible. He promised the workers jobs and security, the employers profits and prosperity, the farmers higher prices for their food and the small shopkeeper protection against the competition of the new chain-stores; he also promised all of them that he would smash the Communist menace.

It was easy to make promises: Hitler's strength was that he persuaded one in three of the German voters that he would carry them out. Already, he argued, it was only the SA which was saving Germany from Communism. By 1932 the SA was four times as large as the German army. Many of its 400 000 members had been recruited from the ranks of the unemployed, put into uniforms, given board and lodging in SA hostels and then sent on to the streets to do battle with the Communists, using anything from knives to knuckledusters. While the Weimar politicians campaigned to have the SA banned because they were a threat to law and order, Hitler boasted that it was only due to their 'heroic activities' that people who were not Communists dared to venture out on the streets.

Above all else, Hitler persuaded 13 million voters that he was the man who would save Germany. Many Germans wanted a strong and dynamic leader whom they could follow without question. This was nothing new in German history. A German publisher wrote in 1758: 'Every nation has its principal motive. In Germany it is obedience: in England freedom'. England had been a powerful nation since 1500; it had not been invaded since 1066. By contrast Germany had not become a nation until 1871. Until then it had been a patchwork of small states straddled across the centre of Europe and as such had been an easy target for invading armies who frequently reduced the lives of the people to misery. As a result, many Germans admired strong rulers such as Frederick the Great and Bismarck who had brought order and unity to the country in the past, and Hitler shrewdly claimed that he was following in their footsteps.

The presidential campaign

Hitler addresses an open-air meeting during the presidential election campaign

The campaign to elect the President in the spring of 1932 gave Hitler the opportunity to convince the voters that he alone had the energy and the will to lead Germany out of its troubles. His main opponent was the 84-year-old President Hindenburg, whose term of office had come to an end. Chancellor Bruning had managed to persuade Hindenburg to stand again, but the old man made only one speech in the entire campaign. The Nazis, by contrast, directed a propaganda campaign such as Germany had never seen before. In the words of an American journalist:

> They plastered the walls of the cities and towns with a million screeching coloured posters ... they staged three thousand meetings a day and, for the first time in a German election, made good use of films and gramophone records [of Nazi speeches], the latter spouting forth from loudspeakers on trucks.
>
> W. Shirer: The Rise and Fall of the Third Reich, 1964

All this frantic activity was not enough for Hitler to win, but it did stop Hindenburg from gaining the absolute majority of votes that he needed, with the result that they had to fight a second election. This time, Hitler chartered an aeroplane which flew him across Germany, enabling him to make speeches before huge crowds in three or four different cities a day. 'For a week,' recalled an observer, 'Germany listened to Hitler.' At the end of it, Hindenburg was re-elected as President after gaining more than 50 per cent of the votes, but Hitler had increased his own vote by more than two million.

The Reichstag elections

Since 1930 the Nazis had been the second largest party in the Reichstag (the German parliamentary assembly). Shortly after the presidential elections they were given a chance to improve on that, as

Hindenburg ordered fresh Reichstag elections to be held in July 1932. He hoped that Chancellor von Papen, who had replaced Bruning, would gain enough support after the elections to get his measures passed through the Reichstag. It was, however, a risky move. Would the voters give the Nazis and the Communists more seats and therefore more chance of bringing down the Weimar Republic?

Using the evidence: the elections of July 1932

A   *I drove back to Berlin to witness the great Grunewald Stadium rally which was to wind up the entire campaign . . . by the time night began to steal over the field, more than a hundred thousand people had paid to squeeze inside, whilst another hundred thousand packed a nearby race-track where loudspeakers had been set up to carry Hitler's words. And at home millions were waiting at the radio, open to the Nazis for the first time in this campaign. Inside the stadium, the stage-setting was flawless . . . banners were silhouetted against the darkening sky . . . twelve huge SA bands played military marches with beautiful precision and terrifying power. Behind the bands on the field itself solid squares of uniformed men were ranged in strict military order, thousands strong.*

Suddenly a wave surged over the crowd . . . Hitler is coming! Hitler is here! A blare of trumpets rent the air and a hundred thousand people leapt to their feet in tense expectancy. All eyes were turned towards the stand, awaiting the approach of the Führer. There was a low rumble of excitement and then the crowd burst into a tremendous ovation, the 'Heils' swelling until they were like the roar of a mighty cataract.

Kurt Ludecke: *I knew Hitler*, 1938

Election meetings frequently ended in violence. Here the police arrive after the damage has been done

B   *According to official statistics, there were between 1st June and 20th July in Prussia, excluding Berlin, 322 serious clashes involving 72 deaths and 497 injured . . . . In Saxony the Communists appeared to have been chiefly responsible . . . the scene of the most disgraceful outrages was, as might be expected, East Prussia, now the stronghold of the National Socialist Party . . . prominent Socialists and Communists were surprised at night and murdered in their beds or shot down at the doors of their houses. The windows of shops owned by Jews were smashed and their contents looted whilst attacks with high explosives were directed against the offices of democratically owned newspapers . . . the assailants not only employed firearms and hand grenades, but also had recourse to the use of hydrochloric acid.*

Sir Horace Rumbold, British Ambassador in Berlin, 1932

C   *Nazi view of the Communist threat*

'Fight with us against the Communist terror.' Nazi election poster of July 1932

Freiwillige Arbeitsdienstpflicht der K. P. D.

In uneigennütziger Weise ist man den Bauern
beim Trocknen der Ernte behilflich —

Dem Verkehrswesen und einer rascheren Beförderung
von Reisenden dienen besondere Ausschüsse —

Keine Nachtschicht und keine Überstunde werden
gescheut, um nützliche Gegenstände unter Dach und
Fach zu bringen —

Im Übrigen wird die vaterländische Ertüchtigung
durch fleißiges Scheibenschießen gefördert.

D *Weimar election results, 1928–32*

	May 1928	Sept 1930	July 1932
Totals on register (in millions)	41.2	43.0	44.2
Percentage of voters	75.6	82.0	84.0
Nazi Party seats	12	107	230
Per cent	2.6	18.3	37.4
Nationalist People's Party seats	73	41	37
Per cent	14.2	7.0	5.9
*German People's Party seats	45	30	7
Per cent	8.7	4.5	1.2
*Centre and Catholic Party seats	78	87	98
Per cent	15.1	14.8	15.9
*Liberal Democratic Party seats	25	20	4
Per cent	3.8	3.6	1.0
*Socialist Party seats	153	143	133
Per cent	29.8	24.5	21.6
Communist Party seats	54	77	89
Per cent	10.6	14.3	14.6

*An asterisk indicates the parties which formed the coalition government led by the Socialists between 1928 and 1930. These parties supported the Weimar Republic although the German People's Party became more nationalist and hostile after the death of its leader, Stresemann, in 1929.

radicalism of the right: this refers to the Nazis
radicalism on the left: this refers to the Communists

E *The so-called race of thinkers and poets is hurrying with flags flying towards dictatorship . . . the radicalism of the right has unleashed a strong radicalism on the left. The Communists have made gains almost everywhere . . . the situation is such that more than half the German people have declared themselves against the present state.*

Comment on the election results from the Reich Minister of the Interior, 1932

1 What new methods and inventions did the Nazis make use of to get their message across to the German people in:
a) the presidential elections (see page 15)
b) the Reichstag election of July 1932 (see source **A**)?
Which of these methods do you think would have done most to increase Hitler's support? Give reasons for your answer.
2 How convincing is the evidence from source **B** in demonstrating that the Nazis used widespread violence in the election campaign?
3 In the Nazi election poster (source **C**) describe what the Communists are shown to be doing in each of the pictures. What image or view of the Communists were the Nazis presenting to the voters?

4 Why do you think the Nazis used violence when they claimed to be the party of order and discipline?
5 How do you think the Nazis justified their use of violence to the voters? Use source C to help you answer this question.
6 Compare the figures in source D for the elections of 1928 and 1932, then write down in two columns (i) which parties had an increase in their percentage of the vote, and (ii) which parties had a decrease.
7 The author of source E stated that 'more than half the German people have declared themselves against the present state'. Did the election results in source D support his conclusion?

Hitler becomes Chancellor

Now that the elections had made the Nazis by far the largest party in the Reichstag, Hitler was all the more determined to become Chancellor at the head of a Nazi government. But President Hindenburg was equally determined not to appoint 'the little Bohemian corporal' whose uniformed thugs were causing havoc on the streets. His main adviser, General Schleicher, agreed with him. Schleicher was a clever back-stage intriguer who had persuaded Hindenburg to drop Bruning and appoint von Papen instead. Hindenburg liked Papen and was determined to keep him as Chancellor, even though Papen was a lightweight politician who had little support in the Reichstag. This weakness was shown when the Reichstag passed a vote of no confidence in Papen's government by 513 votes to 32. As a result, in November 1932, the Germans went to the polling booths for the fourth time that year. This time the Nazis lost votes and seats. They were still the largest party in the Reichstag, but they were running out of money and energy, causing Goebbels, the influential head of Nazi propaganda, to write in his diary: 'The future looks dark and gloomy; all chances and hopes have quite disappeared.'

Events quickly proved Goebbels wrong, for by the end of January 1933 Hitler was installed as Chancellor at the head of a coalition government. The key to the dramatic change in Nazi fortunes was Schleicher, who decided to go for the chancellorship himself. Without intending it, he gave Hitler the opening he wanted. After the November elections Schleicher turned on his former ally Papen, telling Hindenburg that Papen had lost the confidence of the army and that there was now a danger of civil war. He claimed that he would be able to form a government with the support of a majority in the Reichstag. Reluctantly, Hindenburg made Schleicher the new Chancellor instead of Papen. Schleicher was Chancellor for only 54 days. Why did Hindenburg change his mind? Why, on 30 January 1933, did he replace Schleicher with Adolf Hitler, the man he had vowed never to appoint as Chancellor?

Using the evidence

All the extracts below were written by people who were in Germany at the time of the events they are describing:

December–January, 1932–3. *The essence of politics in Germany was a duel between Schleicher and Papen. Schleicher had overthrown Papen. Papen wanted to overthrow Schleicher in his turn.*

K. Heiden: *Hitler*, 1936

January 4. (At a secret meeting between Papen and Hitler.) *Von Papen suggested that this new government should, if possible, be led by Hitler and himself. Then Hitler said that if he were elected Chancellor, Papen's followers could take part in his government, if they were willing to support many alterations including the removal of all Social Democrats, Communists and Jews from leading positions in Germany. Von Papen and Hitler reached agreement in principle . . . whereby cooperation might be possible.*

Schröeder, quoted in *Nazism*, vol 1, eds. J. Noakes and G. Pridham, 1983

January 15–17. *These days changed much. Schleicher had not been able to give his government a broad base. His policy of working with the Reichstag had failed.*

K. Heiden: *Hitler*, 1936

January 18. *Hitler insists on being Chancellor. Papen again considers this impossible. His influence with Hindenburg was not strong enough to effect this.*

Ribbentrop, quoted in *Nazism*, vol 1, eds. J. Noakes and G. Pridham, 1983

January 22. *Papen will now press for Hitler as Chancellor.*

Ribbentrop, as above

January 23. *In the morning Papen saw Hindenburg who refused everything.*

Ribbentrop, as above

January 28. *There was a general feeling [among Hindenburg's advisers] that a government under Hitler which included a proportion of ministers who were not National Socialists [Nazis] would be unable to embark on dangerous experiments.*

Rumbold: *Documents on British Foreign Policy, 1919–39*

January 30. *General Schleicher's Cabinet resigned Saturday last [January 28] . . . . It is well known that the President had not forgiven General Schleicher for supplanting*

Herr von Papen, to whom he is greatly attached . . . if the President flouts the overwhelming mass of public opinion by reappointing Herr von Papen as Chancellor, he will start a campaign against himself.

Rumbold, as above

End of January. *Despite Papen's persuasions, Hindenburg was extremely hesitant, until the end of January, to make Hitler Chancellor. He wanted to have Papen again as Chancellor. Papen finally won him over to Hitler with the argument that the representatives of other right-wing parties which would belong to the government would restrict Hitler's freedom of action . . . if the present opportunity were missed, a revolt of the National Socialists and civil war were likely.*

Meissner, quoted in *Nazism*, vol 1, eds. J. Noakes and G. Pridham, 1983

January 30. *Hitler appointed Chancellor and von Papen Vice-Chancellor.*

Ribbentrop, as above

January 31. *President Hindenburg therefore had to seek a Chancellor who would secure for the government a majority in the Reichstag – this explained the choice of Herr Hitler. On the previous occasion Herr Hitler had insisted that not only must he have the Chancellorship but he must choose his own colleagues. On the latter point, he has now given way perhaps as he has realised the difficulties of his own position.*

Rumbold: *Documents on British Foreign Policy, 1919–39*

Information on sources

Heiden German journalist who wrote several books critical of the Nazis.
Schröeder Wealthy Nazi Party member in whose house the secret meeting of 4 January was held.
Ribbentrop Another wealthy Nazi, in whose house many of the talks were held.
Rumbold British Ambassador to Germany.
Meissner Secretary to President Hindenburg.

1   Between 4 January and 30 January, Papen, Hitler and Hindenburg all changed their attitude towards the question of who should be Chancellor and/or on what terms. Draw up a chart which shows the changes that took place:

	Position in early January	Position 30 January
Papen		
Hitler		
Hindenburg		

2   What, according to the extracts, is the main reason that Papen worked so hard to persuade Hindenburg to appoint Hitler as Chancellor?

3   Hindenburg and his advisers were worried about what Hitler might do if appointed Chancellor. What evidence is there in these extracts of the 'dangerous experiments' that Hitler might carry out if there were no checks on his power?

4 In the extract of 31 January, it is suggested that Hitler made concessions because of 'the difficulties of his own position'. Bearing in mind the November election results, what do you think those difficulties were?

5 Using the extracts explain why Hindenburg
   a) was willing to accept Schleicher's resignation as Chancellor
   b) was finally prepared to appoint Hitler as Chancellor.

6 These extracts include evidence from two leading Nazis.
   a) Are there dangers in using this sort of evidence? If so, what are they?
   b) Is it essential for the historian to use this sort of evidence? Give reasons for your answer.
   c) How might the historian check whether this evidence is reliable or not?

7 Do the extracts strengthen or weaken the view that Hitler was bound to achieve power, given the fact that the Nazis were by far the largest political party in Germany? Explain your answer.

Conclusion

The Depression had created the conditions for Hitler's rise to power. Hitler appealed to people's fears and hates and these emotions flourished in the hard times of the early 1930s. But Hitler's own remarkable talents were crucial to his success. A brilliant master of the dark arts of propaganda, it was he who turned the Nazis into a party of the masses. Then, with a display of ruthless determination to succeed at all costs, he outmanoeuvred the politicians around the President. They were confident that he was under their control when he was appointed Chancellor, but (as we shall see in the next chapter) within two months they, along with the rest of Germany, were under his control.

But what of the majority of Germans who never voted for the Nazis? The Nazis had made it clear they would destroy democracy and all who stood in their way. Why then didn't their enemies join together to stop Hitler? Under the system of proportional representation, where political parties gained seats in direct proportion to the number of votes they received, it was difficult for any one party to gain an absolute majority of seats in the Reichstag. Had the Communists and Socialists joined forces, they would probably have been strong enough both in the Reichstag and on the streets to have blocked the Nazis. But the Communists looked upon the Socialists, not the Nazis, as their main enemy as they struggled with them for the support of the working class. Whereas the Socialists supported the Weimar Republic, the Communists, like the Nazis, wanted it destroyed. The fact was that by 1932–3 there were simply not enough Germans who believed in democracy and individual freedom to save the Weimar Republic.

3 THE NAZI TAKE-OVER OF GERMANY

On the night of 30 January 1933, Adolf Hitler stood at the window of the Chancellery building in Berlin, acknowledging the cheers of thousands of his uniformed supporters who marched past carrying torches and shouting, 'Heil, Heil, Sieg Heil'. Hitler was Chancellor of Germany, but he was not in absolute control of the government. There were only two other Nazis in the Cabinet of 12 ministers, making von Papen, the Vice-Chancellor, confident enough to predict that within two months 'we'll have pushed Hitler into a corner, and he can squeal to his heart's content'. But it was Papen who was left in the corner as Hitler ruthlessly swept his rivals aside.

The Reichstag fire

Once Hitler was Chancellor he insisted on new Reichstag elections. Goebbels wrote in his diary:

> *Now it will be easy to carry on the fight as we can call on all the resources of the State. Radio and press are at our disposal. We shall stage a masterpiece of propaganda.*

The police force of Prussia, by far the largest state in Germany, was also at the disposal of the Nazis because Göring, one of the Nazis in the Cabinet, was Minister of the Interior for Prussia. He drafted in 50 000 extra police mainly from the ranks of the Nazi Party and gave them a free hand to attack their opponents.

Nazis celebrating in Berlin on the night Hitler became Chancellor

The Reichstag in flames

Then a week before the election the Reichstag went up in flames. A Dutch Communist named van der Lubbe was found stripped to the waist inside the burning building. This, Hitler argued, was final proof that the Communists had started their revolution to seize power. That night 4000 Communist leaders were arrested and the following morning Hitler persuaded Hindenburg to sign an emergency decree giving the police the power to search houses, tap telephones, ban meetings and close down newspapers in the interest of national security. A German reporter described how the SA took advantage of the situation:

> *In truckloads they thundered through cities and villages, broke into houses, arrested their enemies at dawn, dragged them out of bed into SA barracks where the victims were frequently beaten to death and their bodies concealed in the woods or thrown into rivers and ponds.*
>
> K. Heiden: *Hitler*, 1936

The Enabling Law

In the last week before the election, the opposition parties were browbeaten into virtual silence as Goebbels's propaganda campaign reached its climax. Not surprisingly the Nazis polled their largest ever number of votes – over 17 million. With the support of the Nationalists they now had a majority in the Reichstag, but it was a bare majority of just over 51 per cent. Hitler was determined to push an Enabling Law through the Reichstag which would give his Cabinet the power to make laws without the approval of the Reichstag or the President. Since that meant altering the Weimar Constitution, it had to be passed with a two thirds majority. There was no opposition from the Communists as most of their elected deputies were already under arrest. The Nazis put the other parties under intense pressure to vote for the Enabling Law. A Socialist deputy describes what happened:

Kroll Opera House: the temporary Reichstag building

SS: Hitler formed the blackshirted SS in 1923 to act as his own bodyguard. In 1933 it had 30 000 members

> *The wide square in front of the Kroll Opera House was crowded with dark masses of people. We were received with wild choruses: 'We want the Enabling Act'. Youths with swastikas on their chests eyed us insolently, blocked our way, in fact made us run the gauntlet, calling us names like 'Centre Pig', 'Marxist Sow'. The Kroll Opera House was crawling with armed SA and SS men ... [during Hitler's speech] we tried to dam the flood of his unjust accusations with interruptions of 'No!', 'An error!', 'False!'. But that did us no good. The SA and the SS people who surrounded us in a semicircle along the walls of the hall, hissed loudly and murmured: 'Shut up!', 'Traitors!', 'You'll be strung up today'.*
>
> Quoted in *Nazism*, vol 2, eds. J. Noakes and G. Pridham, 1984

Of the opposition parties present only the Socialists voted against the Enabling Law which was passed by 444 votes to 94. The Reichstag had, in effect, voted itself out of existence. It met 12 more times in the six years before the war, when it held no debates and listened only to speeches made by Hitler.

Hitler wasted no time in using his new powers to crush the opposition. The Nazis banned all trade unions and German workers had to join the German Labour Front which was under Nazi control. This was followed in July 1933 with a ban on all other political parties. Many opposition leaders were rounded up and sent off to the hastily erected concentration camps which were manned by the SA.

This photo, taken in 1931, shows Hitler standing over Röhm with Göring on the right

The Night of the Long Knives

Now that Hitler was master of Germany there was not enough work to occupy the SA whose numbers had swelled to more than two million by the spring of 1934. Their leader, Ernst Röhm, was pressing Hitler to carry out a second revolution by creating a new People's Army consisting of the SA and the regular army under Röhm's leadership. The army vigorously opposed this and demanded that Hitler deal with Röhm.

Hitler came down in favour of the army: he needed an efficient military force to carry out his foreign policy and, besides, Röhm was a threat to his own authority as sole ruler of Germany.

Hitler decided to strike whilst the SA leaders were holidaying in a lakeside hotel near Munich. In the early hours of 30 June he flew to Munich, from where he was driven in a SS convoy to the hotel. He burst into Röhm's bedroom and arrested him in his pyjamas. Röhm and other SA officers were taken away and later shot. Meanwhile in

Berlin, Göring and Himmler (the leader of the SS) had rounded up 150 SA leaders and put them in a coal cellar in the Cadet School outside the city. They were taken out in fours at 15 minute intervals, lined up against a wall and shot by relays of SS firing squads.

Altogether several hundred people were killed in what was called the Night of the Long Knives. Many of them had nothing to do with the SA. They were on the hit list because at some stage they had annoyed or upset Hitler and his henchmen.

Shortly after the army leaders had thanked Hitler for suppressing the SA, he demanded his reward from them. On 2 August 1934 Hindenburg finally died and within three hours of his death it was announced that Hitler had taken over the Presidency. He was now Head of State and Commander of the armed forces. All officers and soldiers had to swear an oath of absolute obedience to 'Adolf Hitler, the Führer of the German nation and people'. In addition, the fanatically loyal Himmler and his blackshirted SS now replaced the SA as the real power behind Hitler's Reich. It was no wonder that Hitler felt confident enough to say, 'there will be no other revolution in Germany for the next one thousand years'.

Using the evidence: the British Press and the Night of the Long Knives

A *News Chronicle*, 2 July 1934

HITLER'S WEEKEND OF RUTHLESS SLAUGHTER: ARMY NOW IN CONTROL

By ruthless shooting, Hitler and Göring, aided by the Reichswehr (the Regular Army), have quelled what they describe as a "second revolution" in Germany.

In addition to seven Storm Troop leaders shot on Saturday, ten more were executed yesterday.

Captain Röhm, deposed from leadership of the Storm Troops because of his part in the "plot," was shot yesterday after being offered and refusing the opportunity to commit suicide.

Rejecting the revolver held out to him—by Hitler himself, it is stated—he is reported to have declared:

"I will never use this. If I am shot, it must be by Hitler himself."

Apart from the execution of Röhm, yesterday was comparatively quiet in Germany after a week-end of ruthless slaughter in which the victims included ex-Chancellor General von Schleicher and his wife.

Many More Victims
There is every reason to believe that the number of shootings was greater than the public has yet been allowed to know.

The "News Chronicle" learns that the victims also included:

Herr Klausner, a prominent Roman Catholic leader, shot dead by Nazi Guards;

Herr von Bose, chief private secretary and intimate friend of Vice-Chancellor von Papen, who, when the Guards invaded the Vice-Chancellor's room, made a gesture of resistance.

Herr Gregor Strasser, the former Nazi leader, who broke with Hitler on the eve of his attainment to power, murdered — by whom is not clear. Herr Strasser, brother of a prominent Communist, was a leader of the Left section.

In addition, several police officials are believed to have been executed.

Herr von Papen is being kept a prisoner in his own house "under surveillance." Prince August Wilhelm, fourth son of the ex-Kaiser, and a Storm Troop leader, is also reported to be under "protective surveillance."

The attempted revolution is declared to have been a plot between discontented Storm Troop leaders and General von Schleicher, to overthrow the Hitler regime.

A VERY REMARKABLE "PLOT"

It is not likely that the swift disintegration of the Nazi regime will be checked as the result of the spectacular crushing this week-end of the mysterious revolt of the Brown Army leaders concerning which no details have yet been vouchsafed by the authorities.

Nazism is discredited among large sections of the German people although its dramatic collapse is not yet to be expected.

Since early yesterday, when the German public was told of the Munich "mutiny," desperate efforts have been made by Dr. Goebbels, the Minister of Propaganda, to re-establish Hitlerism in the mind of the people upon a new foundation.

Hitler in a new guise

The Chancellor is hailed as the man who came forward to rescue the German people from its Brown Shirt oppressors, while the second rôle ascribed to him is that of the "moral purifier."

Will the enthusiasm of the first phase of the Nazi movement be renewed on grounds such as these?

Will a new Hitler legend come to be substituted for the one that is foundering in widespread dissatisfaction and resentment?

It deserves to be pointed out that the quarrel of the bulk of the German nation with the Brown Army, which is admitted in Nazi official documents this week-end, is merely part of their quarrel with the whole Nazi regime, and that the shooting of a handful of Brown Shirt leaders is not likely to affect the larger issue.

Nonchalant plotters

Even this evening the circumstances of the "revolt," "mutiny," or "revolution," as the movement of the Brown Army leaders is variously called in the State-controlled German newspapers—whose humiliating plight has never been so evidenced as it has been to-day—remain extraordinarily obscure, and official efforts at enlightenment on the point have been most unsatisfactory.

The plotters seem to have acted in a singularly nonchalant fashion, ill-suited to their temperaments, and hardly making for the success of their projects.

Thus in one official statement the German public is told that during Friday night the "High Command" of the Brown Army had given the alarm to the Munich troops.

Yet early on Saturday morning the Chancellor himself found Captain Röhm, Chief of Staff, and Heines, the notorious Breslau murderer, in bed, in Röhm's country home in Bad Wiesec.

Another of the rebels who, it is stated, was shot in trying to escape, Karl Ernst, the Berlin Brown Army Commander, was rounded-up, not at the scene of the plot, but at Bremen, where with his wife and his adjutant he was about to board the steamer Oratawa, for Madeira for—according to one report—a month's holiday in that salubrious island.

That there was much discontent in the Brown Army and in other Nazi organisations is not to be doubted, but what did the Storm Troop leaders aim at, and who were their allies—if they had any?

B *Daily Mail*, 2 July 1934

WHY HITLER SWOOPED: MIDNIGHT DISCLOSURES

HERR ADOLF HITLER, the German Chancellor, has saved his country.

Swiftly and with inexorable severity he has delivered Germany from men who had become a danger to the unity of the German people and to order in the State.

With lightning rapidity he has caused them to be removed from high office, to be arrested, and put to death.

The names of the men who have been shot by his orders are already known, and another list is awaited.

Hitler's love of Germany has triumphed over private friendships and fidelity to comrades who had stood shoulder to shoulder with him in the fight for Germany's future.

He has acted with the knowledge that the best men in Germany desire to see the country purged of those whose influence was evil and whose plots were a perpetual danger.

President von Hindenburg had himself made it plain that stern action must be taken. And in acting Hitler knew that he had the army behind him.

To-day there is rejoicing in Germany as if the nation had wakened from a nightmare. A fresh wind is blowing through the land. Never in the history of our Continent has a ruler cut down the mighty with such dramatic swiftness. Hitler's purge was accomplished in a few hours.

He has stamped out a conspiracy to supplant the present regime.

Herr Hitler flew through the early hours of yesterday morning from the Rhine to Bavaria and himself roused the ringleader, Captain Röhm, Chief of Staff of the Brown Army and Reich Minister without portfolio, from sleep and caused him and his fellow conspirators to be arrested.

Röhm was put in a prison cell and a loaded revolver placed at his side.

Whether from religious convictions or a hope that he might be reprieved at the last moment, he refused to take his life and was shot today.

THE REBEL PLOT DISCLOSED

News which has just come into my possession throws an entirely new light on Saturday's tragic events.

I have received the following details of the great plot which was discovered and which led Herr Hitler to take measures of so violent a nature.

What Hitler had discovered was that the leaders of the Storm Troops with Captain Röhm at the head were conspiring with the leaders of the Army to overthrow his Government, to drive him from power, and to take the direction of Germany into their own hands.

C

'They salute with both hands now.' Low's cartoon of the Night of the Long Knives. Goebbels is crawling between Hitler's legs with Göring on his right

1 What is the main point on which both newspaper accounts agree in their reports on the Night of the Long Knives?

2 Explain with examples how the newspaper accounts disagree in their interpretation of:
   a) the alleged SA plot to overthrow Hitler
   b) the popularity of Hitler within Germany.

3 What point is the cartoonist making when he uses the caption 'They salute with both hands now'?

4 Is the cartoonist more in agreement with the News Chronicle or the Daily Mail? How can you tell?

5 Why do you think that the different newspapers give such different views of the Night of the Long Knives?

6 Had television broadcasting been in existence in 1934, would it have given a fairer and more unbiased view of what happened? Give reasons for your answer.

7 Would you expect history books written in the 1980s to agree about their view of the Night of the Long Knives, or would they be as different as the newspaper accounts? Explain your answer.

4 GERMANY UNDER THE NAZIS

The new Germany

On 1 August 1936, in brilliant sunshine, 110 000 people waited expectantly in what was then the world's largest stadium in Berlin. A fanfare of trumpets sounded and a mighty roar went up from the crowd as Adolf Hitler appeared in the arena and took his place on the platform. He had come, not to address a rally of the Party faithful, but to open the Olympic Games. For the next fortnight Nazi Germany was on display to the world. By the time that the Games ended Hitler had swallowed his anger over an American Negro athlete, Jesse Owens, winning four gold medals. Germany had won more gold medals than any other nation and it appeared that most of the foreign visitors were going home impressed with what they had seen. Certainly David Lloyd George, the former British Prime Minister, was impressed with his visit a few months later: 'The old trust him [Hitler] and the young idolise him ... it is the worship of a national hero who has saved his country from utter despondency and degradation.' Another British Member of Parliament reported that under the Nazis 'tuberculosis and other diseases have noticeably diminished. The criminal courts have never had so little to do and the prisons have never had so few occupants'.

German workers take part in a sack race on a cruise to Madeira. Package holidays were all part of the programme of cheap leisure activities provided by the Nazis to win over the workers

Within three years it seemed that Hitler had restored to the German people their pride and self-respect as a nation. At the time of the Games, one million Germans were out of work compared with six million when Hitler became Chancellor. As he had promised before he came to power, he had swept aside the Treaty of Versailles, increasing his army to 550 000 in 1935 and sending troops into the Rhineland a year later. What was more, he had convinced the British government and Lloyd George along with many others that he was a man of peace.

In reality, however, Hitler was preparing Germany for a war of conquest in Europe. At a top secret conference in 1937, he told his military commanders that the German people needed *Lebensraum*, or living space, beyond the borders of Germany in Eastern Europe, and that the Nazis must be prepared to use force to obtain it. The Nazi government borrowed large sums of money and spent it on purchasing weapons, building airfields, autobahns and docks, and training soldiers, all of which helped to create more jobs. In 1936 Göring was put in charge of the Four Year Plan, whose aim was to make Germany ready for war by 1940 with the country producing all its own food and raw materials. The Plan was not a complete success. When Germany declared war on Poland in 1939, it was still importing 33 per cent of its raw materials and 20 per cent of its food. However, the Plan had put large numbers of people back to work by investing heavily in chemical firms such as I.G.Farben, which had discovered how to produce synthetic rubber and how to refine petrol from coal. By the outbreak of war unemployment was down to 34 000. The price to pay for this success was a large national debt which had risen by 250 per cent between 1933 and 1939. This did not bother Hitler: when his armies overran the Slavs in Eastern Europe, the Slavs would pay Germany's debts.

Heinrich Himmler, leader of the SS

The Nazi police state

There was no room in Hitler's Germany for critics of Nazi rule, except behind the barbed wire of the concentration camps. Germany quickly became a police state in which the security forces of the SS and the Gestapo (the secret police) had sweeping powers to root out and destroy all opposition. The head of the SS, Himmler, and his formidable deputy Heydrich, presided over a vast network of informers who sent in weekly reports from schools, factories, offices and apartment blocks. One Socialist agent reported that:

Members of the illegal movement can hardly meet in people's flats anymore ... every staircase has an informer.
Quoted in *Nazism*, vol 2, eds. J. Noakes and G. Pridham, 1984

The Nazis set up special courts to try their opponents. The judges and, in many cases, the defence lawyers, were loyal Nazis. The guilty were usually sent to the concentration camps, which were manned after 1934 by the Death's Head Units drawn from the most brutal elements of the SS. Conditions in the camps were harsh and punishments were savage. The penalty for discussing politics or merely loitering with other inmates was death.

Even the rare individuals who were found not guilty of political offences were not safe. The wife of one lawyer (who was anti-Nazi) described how outside the court her husband turned to wave goodbye to his client who had been acquitted on the charge of distributing political leaflets:

> *He was just in time to see his client being marched away between two uniformed guards and bundled into a green van. He spent the day making fruitless inquiries ... official shoulders had been shrugged. Had he not heard that in the interests of security there now existed such a thing as protective security .... Peter's client had vanished without trace.*
>
> C. Bielenberg: *The Past is Myself*, 1984

The attack on the churches

Hitler had wasted no time in dealing with his political opponents. Opposition from the churches was more difficult to handle as Hitler could not declare all-out war on Christianity when so many Germans were Roman Catholics or Protestants. In fact, Hitler despised the Christian religion. The Old Testament was the story of the Jewish

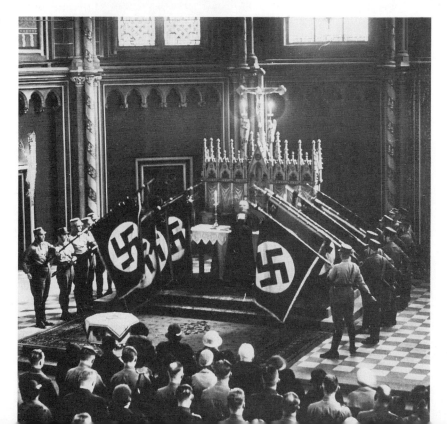

The swastika and the cross: Nazi banners paraded at the altar during the funeral of a Party member

people, while the New Testament message of Christ, himself a Jew, was one of love for all members of the human race. 'We will have no other God but Germany,' thundered Hitler, making it clear that the duty of the churches was to support Nazi rule, not to criticise it.

In years to come worshippers in the churches would listen to readings from *Mein Kampf* and bow before the swastika, but for the present Hitler pretended that he had no quarrel with the churches as long as they did not interfere with Nazi rule.

In July 1933 Hitler signed an agreement with the Pope, whereby it was agreed that the Catholic church would operate freely provided its members did not become involved in politics. Hitler openly broke the agreement by closing down Catholic schools and youth clubs and arresting thousands of priests on trumped up charges of smuggling and sexual immorality.

Hitler tried to take over the Protestant church in Germany directly when he got his own candidate, a member of the German Christian movement of fanatical Nazi supporters, elected as Bishop of the Reich. Some Protestants, inspired by the World War I U-boat captain Martin Niemöller, broke away to form their own church. In his last sermon before being arrested in 1937, Niemöller urged his congregation 'to obey God rather than man'. Along with thousands of other Protestant ministers, Niemöller was sent to a concentration camp where he remained until he was freed by the Allies in 1945. Hitler had made sure that the churches could not lead any effective resistance to Nazi rule, but he had not destroyed the independent spirit of many Christians.

The attack on the Jews

Central to Hitler's vision of the new Germany was a nation rid of its Jewish population. For all his obsessive outpourings about the threat from the Jews, Hitler had no clear master plan for dealing with them. The first move came in 1933 when the Jews were excluded from the civil service, the media and teaching. Two years later the Nuremberg Laws forbade Jews to marry Aryans (a term used by the Nazis to describe non-Jewish Germans) or to have any sexual relationship with them. An American journalist in Germany described what was happening to the Jews:

In many a town the Jew found it difficult if not impossible to purchase food. Over the doors of the grocery and butcher shops, the bakeries and the dairies were signs, 'Jews not admitted'. In many communities Jews could not procure milk even for their young children. Pharmacies would not sell them drugs or medicines. Hotels would not give them a night's lodging. And always, wherever they went, were the taunting signs, 'Jews strictly forbidden in this town', or 'Jews enter this place at their own risk'.

Surrounded by Nazis, two Jews are forced to wear placards saying they are swine who must only associate with other Jews

By 1938 one third of the Jewish population had left Germany, many of them penniless after they had been forced to hand over everything to their Nazi persecutors. Those who remained suffered the full brunt of Hitler's revenge after a Polish Jew shot a German official dead in Paris in 1938. Hitler's supporters took to the streets armed, according to the American Consul, with 'hammers, axes, crowbars and incendiary bombs'. They smashed or set on fire Jewish houses, shops and synagogues and killed several Jews in the orgy of destruction that became known as 'The Night of Broken Glass'. By 1939 the Nazi leaders had decided that they would rapidly clear Germany of the Jews who remained. How this would be done had yet to be decided.

Building the new Germany

As well as silencing his opponents, Hitler was also building the new Reich: the community of German people disciplined and ready to sacrifice themselves on the orders of their leader for the greater glory of the nation. As Minister of Propaganda, Goebbels used all the resources of the powerful Nazi-controlled state to create this new society. He decided what the German people should read in their books and newspapers, what they should listen to on the radio and what they should see when they went to art galleries, cinemas or theatres. Books were burnt and paintings were destroyed if they offended Nazi values. Goebbels made particular use of the radio and the cinema for propaganda purposes. He encouraged manufacturers to produce cheap radios and broadcast Hitler's speeches to the nation, while all cinema programmes contained an up-dated, 45-minute newsreel, which boasted of Nazi achievements.

The ideal mother in Nazi Germany

Hitler Youth on a cross-country run

The indoctrination of the young

The young people of Germany were the main target of the Nazis. If the Reich were to last for a thousand years, Hitler had to win over and control the minds of the young. Goebbels hammered home the message that it was the duty of every German girl to marry and produce a large family of children who would serve the state. The government awarded fertile mothers with medals: the bronze cross for four children, the silver for six and the gold for eight. From the baby's first story book, the German mother was expected to be training her son to be a soldier and her daughter to be the mother of a soldier. The Nazis rewrote the standard nursery rhymes:

> *What puffs and patters?*
> *What clicks and clatters?*
> *I know what. O what fun!*
> *It's a lovely Gatling Gun.*

The Nazis took over the leisure time of the young through the Hitler Youth movement. Boys joined at the age of six and girls at ten. They spent much of their time outdoors with both boys and girls in their separate organisations going on hikes, route marches and camping expeditions. The young were trained to obey and carry out orders, as one former member of Hitler Youth recalled:

> *From childhood onward we were drilled in toughness and blind obedience. At the command 'down', we had to throw ourselves with bare knees onto the gravel; when we were doing press ups our noses were pushed into the sand; anyone who got a stitch cross-country running was ridiculed as a weakling. How did we put up with that for four years? .... Those who did well were promoted, could put on stripes and braid, could give orders even if only for the five minutes when the leader disappeared behind the bushes. Youth must be led by youth was the motto. In practice, that meant that those on top could put the boot in.*
> Quoted in *Nazism*, vol 2, eds. J. Noakes and G. Pridham, 1984

Despite the fact that children were under intense pressure to join the Hitler Youth, in 1938 4.4 million of Germany's total youth population of 12.1 million had not joined. In 1939 membership was made compulsory.

The Nazis soon turned the schools into instruments of indoctrination. A British teacher working in Germany in 1933 reported that:

> *Nazis were sent to schools, where they walked into the classes and cross-examined the teacher in front of his pupils. If they thought it necessary they arrested him at once.*

The schools were plastered with pictures of Adolf Hitler, and all the teachers had to join the Nazi Teachers' League and put across the Nazi message when teaching their own subject.

Using the evidence: indoctrination in the classroom

A *Up till now the religious lessons have consisted for the most part of talks about Herr Hitler and the glories of Germany. Children told me that the teacher had said that Hitler was the second Jesus but greater than the first ... the teacher asks leading questions such as 'Who at the present day reminds us most strongly of Jesus by his love of the people and self-sacrifice?' to which the answer is 'Herr Hitler', and 'Who reminds us by their loyalty and devotion of the Disciples?' The answer: 'General Göring and Dr Goebbels.'*

Vivian Ogilvie: *Experiences of a British Teacher in Germany*, 1934

B *A year's course for senior secondary school pupils.*

Weeks	Subject	Relations to the Jews	Reading Material
1.–4.	Pre-war Germany, The class-war, profits, strikes.	The Jew at large!	Hauptmann's *The Weavers*.
5.–8.	From agrarian to industrial state. Colonies.	The peasant in the claws of the Jews!	Descriptions of the colonies from Hermann Löns.
9.–12.	Conspiracy against Germany, encirclement, barrage around Germany.	The Jew reigns! War plots.	Beumelburg: *Barrage ... Life of Hindenburg, Wartime Letters*.
13.–16.	German struggle—German want. Blockade! Starvation!	The Jew becomes prosperous! Profit from German want.	Manke: *Espionage at the Front.* War reports.
17.–20.	The stab in the back. Collapse.	Jews as leaders of the November insurrection.	Pierre des Granges: *On Secret Service in Enemy Country.* Bruno Brehm: *That was the End.*
21.–24.	Germany's Golgotha. Erzberger's crimes! Versailles.	Jews enter Germany from the East. Judah's triumph.	Volkmann: *Revolution over Germany.* Feder: *The Jews.* The *Stürmer* newspaper.
25.–28.	Adolf Hitler. National Socialism.	Judah's foe!	*Mein Kampf.* Dietrich Eckart.
29.–32.	The bleeding frontiers. Enslavement of Germany. The Volunteer Corps. Schlageter.	The Jew profits by Germany's misfortunes. Loans (Dawes, Young).	Beumelburg: *Germany in Chains.* Wehner: *Pilgrimage to Paris.* Schlageter—a German hero.
33.–36.	National Socialism at grips with crime and the underworld.	Jewish instigators of murder. The Jewish press.	Horst Wessel.
37.–40.	Germany's youth at the helm! The victory of faith.	The last fight against Judah.	Herbert Norkus. The Reich Party Congress.

C *The Jews are aliens [outsiders] in Germany. In 1933 there were 66 060 000 inhabitants in the German Reich of whom 499 682 were Jews. What is the percentage of aliens in Germany?*

Extract from Nazi school textbook

The author of the following extract recalls a lesson in which his homework had been to produce a detailed family tree. With the help of his worried parents, he invented most of the names to disguise the fact that his family were Russian Jews (according to the family's passport they were stateless):

D *He [the teacher] called me out of the class to demonstrate his ability to define the Aryan race according to the size of a person's skull. Using a strange instrument he made a crooked circle on my head . . . and wrote down numbers. The class watched intently this unusual activity and thereupon he began to make calculations and look things up in his tables . . . finally he turned to the class and reported triumphantly, 'Senger, Alpine type with Eastern strain. A thoroughbred specimen of the Aryan race.' He was very satisfied with this skull-measuring exercise. No wonder! He had studied my mother's family tree very thoroughly!*

Valentin Senger, *Kaiserhofstrasse 12*, 1975

1 What subjects do you think were being taught in each of these sources?
2 Write down what you think the Protestant minister Martin Niemöller (p. 32) might have said to his congregation about the Nazi approach to religious education, as described in source **A**.
3 Compare your own current history course with the course in source **B**. Give examples to show in what way the content is similar. What are the most important differences in the way that the subject material is taught? Why are there these differences?
4 What was the teacher in source **D** attempting to prove? Was his experiment successful?
5 The Nazis thought that History, Biology and Physical Education were three of the most important subjects in the timetable. Why do you think they regarded them as so important?
6 Choose any school subject that has not appeared in these sources and suggest how the subject might have been taught in Nazi Germany.
7 Apart from changing what was taught in schools, what else did the Nazis need to do to make their programme of indoctrinating the young successful?

THE EXPANSION OF NAZI GERMANY

When Hitler came to power in 1933, many Germans felt hemmed in by the Treaty of Versailles. The German army was limited to 100 000 men and it had no tanks or aircraft. Millions of German-speaking people were living beyond the borders of the Reich, while the country itself was divided into two. By 1941 Hitler had changed the map of Europe out of all recognition. From Paris in the west to Warsaw in the east the swastika was flying high. As German troops poured into the Soviet Union, Hitler was confident that well before the end of the year the key cities of Moscow, Leningrad and Stalingrad would all be under Nazi control.

Appeasement

Hitler had achieved some of these territorial gains without having to fight. For six years he claimed that all Germany wanted was justice and peace, an army large enough to defend its borders and a Reich that included most of the German-speaking people in Europe. Many people in Britain sympathised with these claims. The mood of the country had changed from demands for revenge after the Great War to feelings of guilt over the harshness of the Treaty of Versailles. Up until the German invasion of Czechoslovakia in March 1939, the British government believed that the best way of avoiding war was to give Hitler what he wanted. Once Germany's reasonable demands had been met, then the risks of war would fade.

This policy of appeasement was actively pursued by Neville Chamberlain, who became Prime Minister in 1937. It was also followed by France, although the French had more serious doubts about what Hitler really wanted. However, they were not prepared to take action against Germany on their own and instead sheltered behind the Maginot line of fortresses built between 1929 and 1934 to deter the Germans from invading France.

Reoccupying the Rhineland

Hitler made his first decisive move in 1936 when he sent his troops across the River Rhine to reoccupy the Rhineland, which was forbidden by the Treaty of Versailles. It was a big gamble on Hitler's part: German forces were still so weak at this stage that they were under orders to withdraw if France sent its troops in. Hitler later said,

German expansion 1936–9

Key:
- Military reoccupation of the Rhineland, 1936
- Austria occupied March 1938
- Sudetenland area of Czechoslovakia occupied October 1938
- Area of Czechoslovakia occupied March 1939

German troops march into the Rhineland. Note the reaction of the onlookers

'The forty-eight hours after the march into the Rhineland were the most nerve-racking in my life'. The French considered taking action, but the British government refused to provide support, arguing that the Germans were 'only going into their own back garden'. Once their troops were back in the Rhineland the Germans rapidly started to fortify the border to block any French invasion. In 1938 Hitler felt secure enough in his own back garden to turn eastwards towards Austria and Czechoslovakia.

In what way is the cartoonist's view of the reoccupation of the Rhineland different from that of the British government?

Union with Austria

Hitler had already tried to take control of Austria in 1934, but he had been stopped by Mussolini, the Fascist dictator of Italy, who was afraid that the German-speaking population of South Tyrol might be encouraged to demand their independence from Italy. By 1938 the two Fascist dictators were allies and Hitler was also confident that Britain and France would not use force to stop the German-speaking people of Austria from joining Hitler's Reich. At his mountain residence at Berchtesgaden, overlooking the Austrian Alps, Hitler told the Austrian Chancellor, Schuschnigg:

> *You certainly aren't going to believe that you can delay me by as much as half an hour. Who knows – perhaps I'll suddenly turn up in Vienna like the spring storm.*

A month later, on 14 March 1938, Hitler did turn up in Vienna, at the head of a large army, announcing to thousands of cheering Austrians 'the entrance of my homeland into the German Reich'. The Jewish population of Austria did not join in the celebrations. William Shirer noted in his diary:

> *On the streets today gangs of Jews with jeering stormtroopers standing over them and taunting crowds around them, on their hands and knees scrubbing the Schuschnigg signs off the sidewalks. Jewish men and women made to clean latrines. Many Jews killing themselves.*
>
> W. Shirer: *Berlin Diary*, 1972

The end of Czechoslovakia?

Shirer went on to predict correctly that 'Czechoslovakia will certainly be next on Hitler's list'. Czechoslovakia was a harder nut to crack than Austria. It had an efficient modern army and was well protected along the German border. Most of its people were not German-speaking and did not want to become part of Germany. It had the support of France and the Soviet Union, who had promised to defend the country if it was attacked. None of this stopped Hitler from telling his generals, 'It is my unalterable decision to smash Czechoslovakia by military action in the near future'.

Hitler started to whip up a campaign among the three million Germans living in the area of Czechoslovakia known as the Sudetenland. He incited them to claim, without justification, that the Czech government was treating them harshly and to demand the right to govern themselves. Hitler expected the Czechs to refuse this demand, thereby losing the support of Britain, France and probably the Soviet Union. This would give Hitler the excuse to seize the whole of the country.

Much depended on what Chamberlain would do. He had three possible courses of action: he could do nothing and allow Hitler to seize the Sudetenland, and perhaps the rest of Czechoslovakia; he could pressure the Czechs to hand over the Sudetenland to Germany on the understanding that Hitler would demand no more territory in Europe; or he could take military action, along with France and Czechoslovakia, to stop Germany from marching into the Sudetenland. Chamberlain thought that Hitler's demands were reasonable: the Sudetenlanders did want to become part of Germany. He was also convinced that he could reach an agreement with Hitler which would bring peace to Europe. That ruled out both the first option of doing nothing and the third option of using force. In addition, the British generals did not want to fight and they told Chamberlain that the army would only be able to supply two divisions which would be 'seriously deficient in modern equipment'.

Chamberlain meets Hitler

Chamberlain, then, decided on the second option of negotiating with Hitler. At their first meeting at Berchtesgaden on 15 September 1938, Hitler demanded the Sudetenland. At their second meeting a week later at Godesberg, Chamberlain told Hitler he could have the Sudetenland. Under intense pressure, the Czechs had agreed to hand it over. Denied the excuse to seize the whole of Czechoslovakia, Hitler increased his demands: the Sudetenland must be handed over by 1 October and parts of Czechoslovakia must be given to Poland and Hungary. This was too much for the British and French governments who now prepared for war. At the last minute, a four power conference was arranged at Munich between Britain, France, Germany and Italy, where it was agreed that the Sudetenland should be handed over by 10 October.

Chamberlain the peace-maker

Afterwards Hitler was annoyed by the settlement, saying 'that fellow Chamberlain has spoiled my entry into Prague'. Meanwhile, Chamberlain was acclaimed as the peace-maker of Europe. *The Daily Telegraph* reported from Germany:

There were scenes of indescribable enthusiasm in the streets of Munich today when Mr Chamberlain left for London. Swastika flags and home-made Union Jacks floated from nearly every window. Almost half the working population seems to have abandoned work for the day to display their gratitude to the man 'who has brought us peace'.

In England cheering crowds greeted Chamberlain as he went from Heston airport to Buckingham Palace and then on to 10 Downing Street. 'I believe this is peace for our time,' he said, waving the agreement he had just signed with Hitler. The Conservative back-bencher Winston Churchill took a different view. Speaking in the House of Commons he described the Munich agreement as a 'total and unmitigated defeat'.

Using the evidence: was Chamberlain right?

A   The argument in the British Cabinet:

[After Chamberlain's first meeting with Hitler] the Prime Minister said it was clearly of the utmost importance to make up one's mind whether the inclusion of the Sudeten Germans was the end at which Hitler was aiming or only the beginning ... the Prime Minister's view was that Hitler was telling the truth. Duff Cooper [First Lord of the Admiralty] expressed the fear that Hitler's promises were quite unreliable.

[After Chamberlain's second meeting with Hitler, the Prime Minister reported that] Herr Hitler had a narrow mind and was violently prejudiced on certain subjects; but he would not deliberately deceive a man whom he respected .... He [Duff Cooper] was certain that our right course of action was to order general mobilisation forthwith. This would make it clear to the German government and might succeed in deterring them from war .... He [Chamberlain] said if we now possessed a superior force to Germany we should probably be considering these proposals in a very different spirit. But we must look facts in the face.

Cabinet minutes, September 1938

B   The debate in Parliament:

The path which leads to appeasement is long and bristles with obstacles .... Now that we have got past the question of Czechoslovakia, I feel that it may be possible to make further progress along the road to sanity.

Neville Chamberlain, as reported in *Hansard*, October 1938

You will find that in a period of time which may be measured by years but may be measured by months, Czechoslovakia will be engulfed by the Nazi regime . . . . The abandonment and ruin of Czechoslovakia is the responsibility of those who have the undisputed control of our political affairs. They neither prevented Germany from rearming, nor did they rearm ourselves in time.

Winston Churchill, as reported in *Hansard*, October 1938

C The view of two German generals:

Had Czechoslovakia defended herself we would have been held up by fortifications in the east, for we did not have the means to break through.

General Manstein, 1946

It was out of the question, with five fighting divisions and seven reserve divisions to hold out against 100 French divisions in the German fortifications in the west [on the border with France] which were nothing but a large construction site.

General Jodl, 1946

D Public opinion:

Mass Observation: a survey of public opinion

After Munich Chamberlain won the approval of 54% of the voters but Mass Observation noted that 'the antis are tending rapidly to build up again'. When asked by the Gallup Poll survey – 'Hitler says he has no more territorial ambitions in Europe. Do you believe him?', 7% said Yes, 93% said No.

E

Crowds outside 10 Downing Street greet Chamberlain on his return from Munich

1 Does the evidence of the German generals in source **C** strengthen or weaken the argument of Duff Cooper (source **A**) in favour of mobilisation? Explain your answer.

2 What evidence is there in these extracts that Chamberlain was becoming less confident about his policy of negotiating with Hitler?

3 In what way does the photograph give a different view of the public reaction to the Munich agreement compared with the surveys of public opinion in source **D**? Which view do you think gives a more accurate picture of public opinion and why?

4 Fill in your own summary chart showing the views of
   a) Chamberlain and his supporters
   b) Chamberlain's opponents in Britain
   towards the topics listed below:

	(a) Pro-Chamberlain	(b) Anti-Chamberlain
1 The military position of both sides		
2 Views about Hitler		
3 The correct British policy to-wards Hitler over the Sudeten-land		
4 Hitler's likely course of action after Munich		

5 In the light of the information available to Chamberlain at the time, do you think that he took the right decision in signing the Munich agreement? Explain your answer.

The coming of war

Chamberlain's policy of appeasement collapsed abruptly in March 1939 when Hitler's troops marched into the rest of Czechoslovakia, bearing out Churchill's prediction that 'Czechoslovakia will be en-gulfed in the Nazi regime'. To prevent further German aggression Britain promised to defend Poland, stepped up its rearmament programme and started to negotiate with the Soviet Union about jointly protecting Poland. But they were unable to reach agreement because neither side could trust the other. Stalin, who was deeply concerned about the threat of a Nazi invasion of the Soviet Union, turned instead to his arch-enemy Hitler and on 23 August the Nazi-Soviet pact was signed. Publicly both countries agreed not to fight each other. Privately they agreed to carve up Poland between them.

On 1 September Germany invaded Poland. Britain and France declared war on Germany but were unable to defend Poland, whose open plains were rapidly overrun by German forces. When the Soviet troops invaded from the east on 17 September, 'there were scarcely any Polish troops left to oppose them'. As the victors divided up their spoils, Hitler was already planning his attack on the west.

The conquest of Western Europe

Hitler had successfully deceived his political opponents during peace-time. He went on to outmanoeuvre the Allied generals during the first stages of the war. In the Great War, the German armies had failed to break the stalemate on the Western Front in four years of fighting. It took Hitler six weeks to conquer the mainland of Western Europe. This success was due, first, to the new tactics of lightning warfare (Blitzkrieg), where Hitler used tanks and aeroplanes to cut through and destroy the enemy defences. Secondly, when Hitler did launch his invasion in May 1940, he caught the Allies by surprise. He launched

Right: *German invasion of Western Europe, 1940*

Below: *A German tank moves into a French town in ruins after bombardment from the air*

Key:
- - - - Maginot line
▨ German advance
▨ Allied territory around Dunkirk at the start of the evacuation

his main tank offensive through the forests of the Ardennes, which the Allies thought were impassable for tanks (see map on page 44). Allied armies had already raced further north to deal with what they thought was the main German offensive. As the German tanks advanced in a 96 kilometre column along the winding roads of the Ardennes, crossed the River Meuse and moved rapidly across the open ground of northern France towards the sea, the Allied armies found themselves trapped within a shrinking triangle of territory.

Dunkirk

Disaster seemed inevitable for the retreating Allies, when suddenly the forward panzer (tank) divisions were halted. Hitler was worried about the number of tanks that were out of action and he was confident that Göring's Luftwaffe (air force) would on its own destroy the Allied armies from the air. But bad weather grounded his aeroplanes and this gave the Allies precious time to evacuate their troops by sea. Altogether 330 000 soldiers were ferried from the beaches to safety in Britain.

Allied troops being evacuated from Dunkirk

Britain stands alone

After Dunkirk the remaining French armies fell back in disarray as the Germans pressed south. The French government had to sign the armistice in the same railway carriage on the same spot where the Germans had signed the armistice in 1918. Hitler had exacted his revenge and he now expected the British to seek peace. Churchill, who had replaced Chamberlain as Prime Minister on the day Hitler invaded Belgium and Holland, pledged the nation to continue the struggle. On 4 June 1940 he told the House of Commons:

> *We shall defend our island whatever the cost may be. We shall fight on the beaches, we shall fight on the landing grounds, we shall fight on the fields and on the streets, we shall fight in the hills; we shall never surrender.*

In fact, the decisive fighting took place in the air. Hitler planned to send 200 000 troops across the Channel in large barges, but first he needed mastery of the air. Göring promised to wipe out the RAF in a month by striking at the radar stations and ring of airfields around London, but just when Britain's position looked desperate Hitler switched from attacking airfields to bombing London in retaliation for a British bombing raid on Berlin. Hitler's hopes that the raids would shatter the morale of the civilian population proved wrong, and the RAF was given enough time to recover and to enable its pilots to inflict heavy losses on the Luftwaffe.

Winston Churchill

Operation Barbarossa

Having failed to gain control of the air, Hitler now planned to starve Britain into surrender by using his U-boats to sink ships bringing vital food supplies into the country. This would take time, but Hitler knew that time was not on his side when it came to the decisive show-down with his main enemy, the Soviet Union. He was confident of an easy victory: 'We have only to kick in the door and the whole rotten structure will come crashing down.' At dawn on 22 June 1941 Hitler launched 'Operation Barbarossa', as three million German troops poured into the Soviet Union. Hundreds of Soviet aeroplanes were destroyed on the ground and entire Soviet armies surrendered as the Germans advanced. To many people German mastery of the entire continent of Europe and beyond seemed only a matter of time.

Above: *German air attack on London, August 1940*

Below: *Nazi control of Europe, 1942*

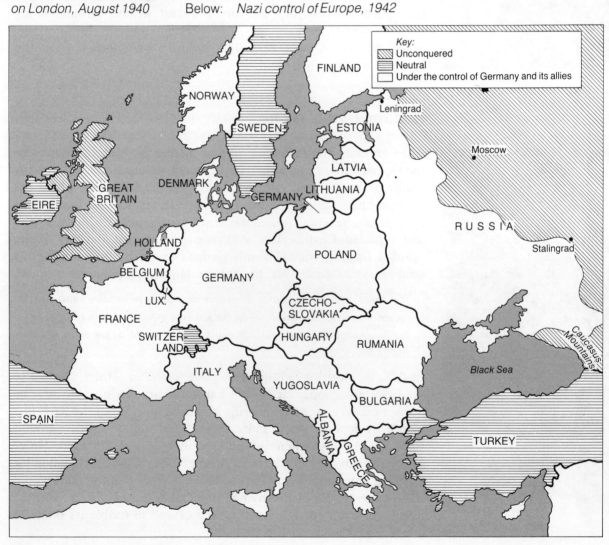

6

NAZI OCCUPATION AND ALLIED VICTORY

When the SS leader Heinrich Himmler found out that his doctor hunted animals for sport, he asked him how he could find pleasure in shooting innocent and defenceless creatures. 'Every animal,' he told the doctor, 'has the right to live.' Himmler did not extend that right to millions of humans living in Nazi-occupied Europe. The SS were the instruments of Hitler's 'New Order'; they were charged with the task of reducing the Slavs of Eastern Europe to the position of slaves working for their Aryan masters, and eliminating the Jews altogether. Himmler prided himself on his clinical efficiency, informing his SS group leaders in 1943:

> *... whether or not 10,000 Russian women collapse from exhaustion while digging a tank ditch interests me only in so far as the tank ditch is completed for Germany.*

Eastern Europe, in particular, captured the twisted imagination of the Nazi leaders. 'The east,' Hitler said, 'has everything in unlimited quantities: iron, coal, oil and a soil that can grow everything that Europe needs.' It also had 'living space' for the German farmers whom Hitler planned to settle in a ring of attractive villages outside the fortified towns.

The first task Himmler gave the SS in Poland and the Soviet Union was to hunt down and kill the leaders of both nations: in Poland this meant the clergy, aristocrats and intellectuals; in the Soviet Union it meant officials of the Communist Party. At the same time the SS rounded up the large Jewish population of both countries. In Poland in 1939 they herded them into ghettos to await their fate. Two years later more than a million Russian Jews were transported in trucks into the countryside where they were shot.

A Jewish mother and child are shot in an open field

The SS also disposed of Russian soldiers and civilians whom they captured. When the German army took control of the city of Kharkov in 1941, its officers decided that they could feed only 150 000 out of the population of 250 000. They handed over the rest to the SS who gave them picks and shovels and ordered them to build a massive trench outside the city. At the end of the day, according to one of the few survivors, an SS lorry drove slowly along the edge of the trench collecting the picks and shovels. It then drove back with SS guards machine-gunning the diggers, followed by a bulldozer which pushed the bodies into the trench.

In territory occupied by the German armies, hundreds of thousands of Russian prisoners were marched to camps and left to starve. A Hungarian officer, fighting for Germany, recalled how he had come across a prisoner-of-war camp:

I woke up one morning and heard thousands of dogs howling in the distance . . . . I called my orderly and said: 'Sandor, what is all that howling and moaning?' 'Not far from here,' he said, 'there is a huge mass of Russian prisoners in the open air. They're moaning because they are starving.' I went to have a look. Behind wire there were tens of thousands of Russian prisoners. Their faces were dried up and their eyes were sunk deep into their sockets. Hundreds were dying every day and those with any strength left dumped them in a vast pit.
Dr Sulyok, quoted in *Purnell's History of the Twentieth Century*,
vol 5, 1969

As the Allies put increasing pressure on Germany in the war, the Nazis decided to put their prisoners to more profitable use in German factories. They worked alongside civilian men and women from all over Europe who had been rounded up, flung into cattle trucks and dispatched to Germany where they were forced to live in overcrowded and unhygienic camps. In May 1944 there were more than seven million foreign workers in Germany, enabling the country to produce three times as many goods as it had produced in 1942.

The Final Solution

Hitler's New Order came closest to chilling fulfilment when the Nazis set in motion their programme to exterminate the Jews. At a meeting held on 20 January 1942, Heydrich told a group of high-ranking officials that the time had come for the 'Final Solution of the European Jewish problem'. After considering various proposals such as exile to Madagascar, the Nazi leaders had chosen genocide. That winter six concentration camps were converted to extermination camps with the building of gas chambers and crematoria. All over Europe Jews were systematically rounded up and sent off in rail trucks to the camps. The largest camp was at Auschwitz in Poland. On arrival the Jews were

genocide: the deliberate extermination of a race

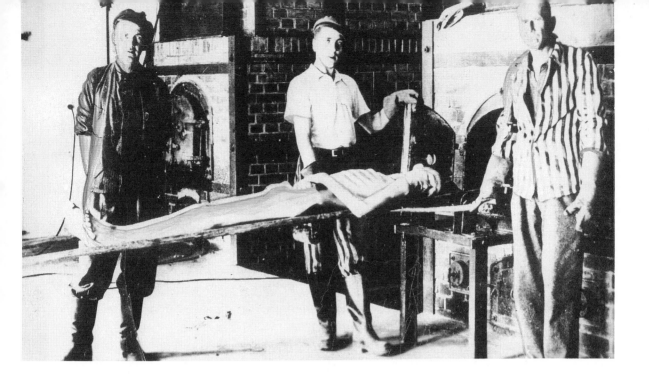

Furnaces at Auschwitz which were used to burn the bodies

divided into two groups: those who were fit to work and those who were not. Loudspeakers informed those who had been judged unfit that they were going to be showered and deloused. A female orchestra played light music as the Jews were marched off to the 'baths'. William Shirer describes what happened after they had undressed:

Once they were inside the 'shower room' – and perhaps this was the first moment that they may have suspected that something was amiss, for as many as two thousand were packed into the chamber like sardines, making it difficult to take a bath – the massive door was slid shut, locked and hermetically sealed. Up above orderlies stood ready to drop into the vents the amethyst-blue crystals of hydrogen cyanide or Zyklon B . . . . Through heavy glass portholes the executioners could watch what happened. The naked prisoners below would be looking up at the showers from which no water spouted or perhaps at the floor wondering why there were no drains. It took some moments for the gas to have much effect. But soon the inmates became aware that it was issuing from the perforations in the vents. It was then that they usually panicked, crowding away from the pipes and finally stampeding towards the huge metal door where as Reitlinger puts it, 'they piled up in one blue clammy blood-spattered pyramid, clawing and mauling each other even in death'.

Reitlinger: a post-war historian

W. Shirer: *The Rise and Fall of the Third Reich*, 1964

In 1941 there were about eight and a half million Jews living in territory occupied by the Nazis. It is estimated that by the end of the war the SS had killed nearly six million of them. In Auschwitz alone two and a half million people, mostly Jews, were gassed and another half million died of starvation or disease.

Using the evidence: Kitty Hart – a survivor of Auschwitz

Total obedience, total humiliation. It was no use trying to predict logically what they would do. Yet at the same time you had to be somehow a step ahead. You had to develop special antennae . . . . Above all keep away from those who said it wasn't worth trying to go on. Despair was contagious. Despair turned you into a Muselmann. There was one period when illness had almost the same awful effect on me. It started with a night when I couldn't sleep, tired as I was. I tossed and turned, hot and shivery, icy cold and then bathed in sweat. Was it typhus? Nearly everyone caught it sooner or later. It was as common a killer as the SS.

[Kitty Hart was then taken to the hospital block where her mother was working.] The block was full. I was put on to a single bunk which already had three occupants. One patient had diphtheria, another malaria and the third had typhus. . . . I heard myself crying for water. Then I must have been unconscious for a long time. Then awake, or half awake, I thought I could see oranges, grapes and cool drinks at the foot of my bunk and screamed for them. Mother was there and I cursed her for being so cruel . . . .

One day as I lay unconscious there was a selection. All those unable to get up were taken to be gassed. Mother saw what would surely happen to me. She pushed me inside a straw mattress and laid a corpse on top of me, praying I would keep still and not start raving and singing, as I had been doing some hours earlier. The SS doctor passed the bunk.

Muselmann: the name given in the camps to those who had given up hope

A view of Auschwitz

*The corpse was taken away. The incurably sick were taken
also. I was still alive . . . .*

*During my convalescence another selection was carried
out. That day I was able to walk, but not very well. Mother was
worried, too, about the sores and scratches on my body. And
I was far too thin. One by one we had to parade naked
outside. Mengele himself was there. He ordered us to run.
Those who could not summon up the energy to run were sent
to the left, the others to the right. I gathered all my strength,
began to run and somehow made it. But Mengele was staring
hard at my pimply body. He made me turn round, then round
again, while he hesitated . . . and at last pointed to the right.*

Kitty Hart: *Return to Auschwitz*, 1981

Mengele: the chief camp
doctor

1 Make a list of all the occasions in this extract when the author
   was near to death.
2 Why did the author manage to survive on these occasions?
   How important were
   a) her own attitude and efforts
   b) the support of her mother
   c) chance and luck?
3 Few Auschwitz inmates who were not gassed on arrival
   survived longer than three months. Use the evidence from this
   extract to explain why it became increasingly difficult to survive
   in the camp.
4 Why do you think that the Nazis were anxious to conceal what
   was happening at the extermination camps both from the
   German public and the wider world?

Allied victory

In less than a year Nazi Germany declared war on the two most
powerful countries in the world. Hitler followed up the invasion of the
Soviet Union in June 1941 with a declaration of war on the United
States on 11 December in support of his ally, Japan, whose airforce
had attacked the US naval base at Pearl Harbour four days earlier.
The massive resources of both the Soviet Union and the USA were
almost certain to defeat Germany and its weak European ally, Italy, if
the war went on for any length of time. Hitler needed a speedy victory
and he was confident that he had achieved it in the Soviet Union,
announcing in October 1941 that 'the enemy in the east has been
struck down and will never rise again'. However, as the German
offensive ground to a halt outside the cities of Leningrad and Moscow,
it became clear that Hitler had gravely underestimated both the Soviet
climate and the Soviet people.

Setback in the east

Leningrad in the north was under siege from the Germans for 890 days. For part of that time, the inhabitants depended for their survival on one hazardous supply route across a frozen lake. Reduced to rations of 120 grams of bread a day and the occasional meat jelly made from sheep gut, nearly one million of the city's population of three million did not survive, but the remainder held out until the siege was finally lifted in January 1944.

Further south, Hitler delayed his attack on Moscow for a vital two-month period in the summer of 1941. He was more concerned with capturing Leningrad in the north and the wheat fields and industrial areas of the Ukraine further south. When the generals finally persuaded him to change his mind it was too late. The attack was slowed down by autumn rains and then virtually halted by the Russian winter in which the temperature commonly dropped to 20 degrees (and at times even 60 degrees) below freezing. Earlier Hitler had been so sure of a quick victory that he had refused to allow winter uniforms to be issued. Now his soldiers paid the price of his over-confidence and many simply froze to death. Within sight of Moscow, the German army was forced to call off its attack on 5 December 1941 and one day later it was driven back by a Soviet counter-offensive.

For the 1942 campaign, Hitler concentrated on the south where he planned to capture the oilfields of the Caucasus, thereby depriving the Soviet army of its supplies of fuel. However, when he also decided to capture the city of Stalingrad, he made the mistake of trying to do too much. The Russians contested the advance of the Sixth Army on the city every step of the way:

In each embattled house, the German dead lay strewn in the cellars and on the landings or were sprawled on the shattered staircases.

According to this Soviet wartime cartoon, who was responsible for the defeat of Hitler?

Inside, the Russians held off the Germans with grenades, automatic fire, bayonets and fighting knives, every room turned into a small fort with weapons poking through firing points ... if the Germans took a part of a building by day, at night the Russians returned, feet bound in sacking to deaden the noise or swinging along the shattered roof-beams, grenades and light weapons at the ready.

J. Erickson: *The Road to Stalingrad*, 1975

Meanwhile two Soviet armies broke through the German lines north and south of Stalingrad and joined up to encircle the Sixth Army, which was now trapped within the city. Defying Hitler's orders to stand and fight to the last man, Paulus, the commander, surrendered on 30 January 1943 and the frostbitten and half-starved remnants of his army were taken prisoner. The campaign had failed: both Stalingrad and the oilfields remained in Soviet hands.

Hitler's final chance of victory in the east came in the summer of 1943 when German forces attacked the Soviet army at Kursk, in the biggest tank battle of the war. But they failed to achieve the breakthrough and from then on the Soviet steamroller gradually forced the Germans back across Eastern Europe. When troops from the Red Army finally reached Hitler's bunker in Berlin on 2 May 1945, the Soviet death toll in the war amounted to 20 million people. With the help of supplies from its western allies, Britain and America, the Soviet Union had blunted the German offensive and shown that German armies could be defeated. It was Churchill who said that 'it was the Russians who tore the guts out of the German army'.

The Battle of the Atlantic

In the west, Hitler's best chance of victory lay in winning control of the Atlantic and thereby preventing essential supplies and food reaching Britain from America. The U-boats were Hitler's main weapon: they travelled fast on the surface by day searching for the Allied shipping convoys, then at night they formed into wolf packs to attack their target. The convoys were particularly at risk in 'the gap', an area several hundred kilometres wide in the north-east Atlantic, where they had no aircraft protection as it was beyond the range of the land bases. By March 1943 the U-boats were sinking so many Allied ships that one commentator later wrote of the British Admiralty:

They must have felt, though no one admitted it, that defeat stared them in the face.

Yet less than two months later, the Battle of the Atlantic had tilted decisively in favour of the Allies. The most important reason for this dramatic change was that the Allies finally succeeded in providing effective air cover for their convoys across the entire Atlantic. The United States government supplied increasing numbers of aircraft carriers and Very Long Range aircraft to protect the convoys on their

Allied air attack sinks a German U-boat

hazardous voyage. Equipped to carry 2 000 gallons of fuel and eight depth charges, the VLR aircraft were able to cover 'the gap'. Along with the destroyers, they were fitted with a new form of short-wave radar which gave them early warning of surfaced U-boats.

Further information about the position of the U-boats came from Allied intelligence officers. In December 1942, after ten months of frustrated effort, they finally cracked the new German naval code which was used to relay radio messages between the U-boats and their base. Armed with guns, depth charges and knowledge of the whereabouts of the U-boats, Allied aircraft, assisted by the naval destroyers, proved too much for their opponents. In less than two months, the U-boat hunters had become the hunted. On 24 May Admiral Donitz withdrew the U-boats temporarily from the Atlantic and the Germans conceded that 'the decision in the Battle of the Atlantic had gone to the enemy'.

Using the evidence: statistics of the battle

1943	Allied ships sunk, in tons	Operational U-boats	U-boats sunk	Operational VLR aircraft
January	200 000	214	6	not known
February	360 000	221	19	14
March	627 000	231	15	not known
April	328 000	237	15	41
May	264 000	239	41	70

1 According to the table, which month was the most critical for the Allies and why?
2 Would you agree with the statement that the Allied position was worse in May than it had been in January because the Allies were losing a greater tonnage of shipping? Give reasons for your answer.
3 Prepare the report that Admiral Donitz might have presented to Hitler explaining why it was necessary to withdraw the U-boats on 24 May. As well as using the table, refer to information in the text and any other relevant material that you can find.

The end of Hitler

With the Atlantic relatively safe for the convoys, the Allies went ahead with full-scale preparations for the invasion of Europe. The United States government shipped soldiers and vast quantities of supplies to Britain, from where Operation Overlord was launched in June 1944. Allied forces landed in Normandy and, aided by their superiority in the air, forced their way into France against determined German

Encirclement of Germany, 1943–5

Key:
→ Western Allied advances
⇨ Soviet advances
〰 Boundaries of Germany after the Treaty of Versailles
–·– Furthest point reached by Allied armies from East and West

Leningrad
•Moscow
Kursk
Berlin
•Stalingrad
Allied landings, June 1944
Paris
Prague
Vienna
Rome
Allied invasions, July 1943

Below: *This photograph was taken in April 1945 in the ruins of the Chancellery building. It is almost certainly the last picture ever taken of Hitler (on the right)*

resistance. Germany relived its 1914 nightmare of encirclement, as their opponents closed in from the west, the east and the south. In November 1944, Hitler was forced to abandon his headquarters in a remote forest in East Prussia and to return to Berlin where he lived out the last few months of his life in an underground concrete bunker.

The once confident and energetic dictator was hardly recognisable. At the age of 56, Hitler walked with a stoop, the left side of his body trembled and saliva trickled out of the corners of his mouth. Since the defeat at Stalingrad Hitler had cut himself off more and more from the war which he had engineered. He refused to listen to bad news and sacked generals who disagreed with him. He avoided visiting the battlefields and the German cities which were under more or less constant attack from the Allied bombers.

With the sound of Soviet gunfire reaching the Chancellery building in Berlin, Hitler was at last forced to recognise that his plans for the New Order had collapsed. In the early hours of 29 April he married his mistress, Eva Braun. In the afternoon he was told that Mussolini had been hung upside-down by his feet outside a garage in Milan. Twenty-four hours later Eva Braun took poison and Hitler shot himself. Their bodies were taken out of the bunker and burnt in the Chancellery garden. The Third Reich had finally been extinguished.

INDEX